M

DATE DUE

DEC 0 9 2007	
DEC 2 8 2007	
JAN 2 3 2008	

DEMCO INC. 38-2931

NOV 0 4 2007

811.54
Pinsk.R

Also by Robert Pinsky

Poetry
Sadness And Happiness (1975)
An Explanation of America (1979)
History of My Heart (1984)
The Want Bone (1990)
The Figured Wheel (1996)
Jersey Rain (2000)

Prose
Landor's Poetry (1968)
The Situation of Poetry (1977)
Poetry and the World (1988)
The Sounds of Poetry (1998)

Translations
The Separate Notebooks, by Czeslaw Milosz (1983)
The Inferno of Dante (1994)

GULF MUSIC

GULF MUSIC

Robert Pinsky

Farrar, Straus and Giroux · New York

Farrar, Straus and Giroux
19 Union Square West, New York 10003

Distributed in Canada by Douglas & McIntyre Ltd.
Printed in the United States of America
First edition, 2007

Some of these poems were first published, sometimes in different form, in magazines. Grateful acknowledgment is made to the editors: *Agni*, *The American Poetry Review*, *The American Scholar*, *The Atlantic*, *The Boston Globe Magazine*, *London Review of Books*, *The Nation*, *The New Republic*, *The New Yorker*, *Ploughshares*, *Poetry*, *Salmagundi*, *The Threepenny Review*, and *The Washington Post Magazine*.

Library of Congress Cataloging-in-Publication Data
Pinsky, Robert.
    Gulf music / Robert Pinsky.— 1st ed.
        p.   cm.
    ISBN-13: 978-0-374-16749-3 (hardcover : alk. paper)
    ISBN-10: 0-374-16749-4 (hardcover : alk. paper)
    I. Title.

PS3566. I54 G86 2007
811'.54—dc22

                                        2007004325

Designed by Jonathan D. Lippincott

www.fsgbooks.com

10   9   8   7   6   5   4   3   2   1

CONTENTS

III

I

Poem of Disconnected Parts

At Robben Island the political prisoners studied.
They coined the motto *Each one Teach one.*

In Argentina the torturers demanded the prisoners
Address them always as *"Profesor."*

Many of my friends are moved by guilt, but I
Am a creature of shame, I am ashamed to say.

Culture the lock, culture the key. Imagination
That calls the boiled sheep heads in the market "Smileys."

The first year at Guantánamo, Abdul Rahim Dost
Incised his Pashto poems into styrofoam cups.

*"The Sangomo says in our Zulu culture we do not
Worship our ancestors: we consult them."*

Becky is abandoned in 1902 and Rose dies giving
Birth in 1924 and Sylvia falls in 1951.

Still falling still dying still abandoned in 2006
Still nothing finished among the descendants.

I support the War, says the comic, it's just the Troops
I'm against: can't stand those Young People.

Proud of the fallen, proud of her son the bomber.
Ashamed of the government. Skeptical.

After the Klansman was found Not Guilty one juror
Said she just couldn't vote to convict a pastor.

Who do you write for? I write for dead people:
For Emily Dickinson, for my grandfather.

"The Ancestors say the problem with your Knees
Began in your Feet. It could move up your Back."

But later the Americans gave Dost not only paper
And pen but books. Hemingway, Dickens.

Old Aegyptius said, Whoever has called this Assembly,
For whatever reason—that is a good in itself.

O thirsty shades who regard the offering, O stained earth.
There are many fake Sangomos. This one is real.

Coloured prisoners got different meals and could wear
Long pants and underwear, Blacks got only shorts.

No he says he cannot regret the three years in prison:
Otherwise he would not have written those poems.

I have a small-town mind. Like the Greeks and Trojans.
Shame. Pride. Importance of looking bad or good.

Did he see anything like the prisoner on a leash? Yes,
In Afghanistan. In Guantánamo he was isolated.

Our enemies "disassemble" says the President.
Not that anyone at all couldn't mis-speak.

The *profesores* created nicknames for torture devices:
The Airplane. The Frog. Burping the Baby.

Not that those who behead the helpless in the name
Of God or tradition don't also write poetry.

Guilts, metaphors, traditions. Hunger strikes.
Culture the penalty. Culture the escape.

What could your children boast about you? What
Will your father say, down among the shades?

The Sangomo told Marvin, *"You are crushed by some*
Weight. Only your own Ancestors can help you."

Gulf Music

Mallah walla tella bella. Trah mah trah-la, la-la-la,
Mah la belle. Ippa Fano wanna bella, wella-wah.

The hurricane of September 8, 1900 devastated
Galveston, Texas. Some 8,000 people died.

The Pearl City almost obliterated. Still the worst natural
Calamity in American history, Woh mallah-walla.

Eight years later Morris Eisenberg sailing from Lübeck
Entered the States through the still-wounded port of Galveston.

1908, eeloo hotesy, hotesy-ahnoo, hotesy ahnoo mi-Mizraim.
Or you could say "Morris" was his name. A Moshe.

Ippa Fano wanna bella woh. The New Orleans musician called
Professor Longhair was named Henry Roeland Byrd.

Not heroic not nostalgic not learnèd. Made-up names:
Hum a few bars and we'll homme-la-la. Woh ohma-dallah.

Longhair or Henry and his wife Alice joined the Civil Defense
Special Forces 714. Alice was a Colonel, he a Lieutenant.

Here they are in uniforms and caps, pistols in holsters.
Hotesy anno, Ippa Fano trah ma dollah, tra la la.

Morris took the name "Eisenberg" after the rich man from
His shtetl who in 1908 owned a town in Arkansas.

Most of this is made up, but the immigration papers did
Require him to renounce all loyalty to Czar Nicholas.

As he signed to that, he must have thought to himself
The Yiddish equivalent of *No Problem*, Mah la belle.

Hotesy hotesy-ahno. Wella-mallah widda dallah,
Mah fanna-well. A townful of people named Eisenberg.

The past is not decent or orderly, it is made-up and devious.
The man was correct when he said it's not even past.

Look up at the waters from the causeway where you stand:
Lime causeway made of grunts and halfway-forgettings

On a foundation of crushed oyster shells. Roadbed
Paved with abandonments, shored up by haunts.

Becky was a teenager married to an older man. After she
Met Morris, in 1910 or so, she swapped Eisenbergs.

They rode out of Arkansas on his motorcycle, well-ah-way.
Wed-away. "Mizraim" is Egypt, I remember that much.

The storm bulldozed Galveston with a great rake of debris.
In the September heat the smell of the dead was unbearable.

Hotesy hotesy ahnoo. "Professor" the New Orleans title
For any piano player. He had a Caribbean left hand,

A boogie-woogie right. Civil Defense Special Forces 714
Organized for disasters, mainly hurricanes. Floods.

New Orleans style borrowing this and that, ah wail-ah-way la-la,
They probably got "714" from Joe Friday's badge number

On *Dragnet.* Jack Webb chose the number in memory
Of Babe Ruth's 714 home runs, the old record.

As living memory of the great hurricanes of the thirties
And the fifties dissolved, Civil Defense Forces 714

Also dissolved, washed away for well or ill—yet nothing
Ever entirely abandoned though generations forget, and ah

Well the partial forgetting embellishes everything all the more:
Alla-mallah, mi-Mizraim, try my tra-la, hotesy-totesy.

Dollars, dolors. Callings and contrivances. King Zulu. Comus.
Sephardic ju-ju and verses. Voodoo mojo, Special Forces.

Henry formed a group named Professor Longhair and his
Shuffling Hungarians. After so much renunciation

And invention, is this the image of the promised end?
All music haunted by all the music of the dead forever.

Becky haunted forever by Pearl the daughter she abandoned
For love, O try my tra-la-la, ma la belle, mah walla-woe.

Keyboard

A disembodied piano. The headphones allow
The one who touches the keys a solitude
Inside his music; shout and he may not turn:

Image of the soul that thinks to turn from the world.
Serpent-scaled Apollo skins the naive musician
Alive: then Marsyas was sensitive enough

To feel the whole world in a touch. In Africa
The raiders with machetes to cut off hands
Might make the victim choose, "long sleeve or short."

Shahid Ali says it happened to Kashmiri weavers,
To kill the art. There are only so many stories.
The Loss. The Chosen. And even before The Journey,

The Turning: the fruit from any tree, the door
To any chamber, but this one—and the greedy soul,
Blade of the lathe. The Red Army smashed pianos,

But once they caught an SS man who could play.
They sat him at the piano and pulled their fingers
Across their throats to explain that they would kill him

When he stopped playing, and so for sixteen hours
They drank and raped while the Nazi fingered the keys.
The great Song of the World. When he collapsed

Sobbing at the instrument they stroked his head
And blew his brains out. Cold-blooded Orpheus turns
Again to his keyboard to improvise a plaint:

Her little cries of pleasure, blah-blah, the place
Behind her ear, lilacs in rain, a sus-chord,
A phrase like a moonlit moth in tentative flight,

O lost Eurydice, blah-blah. His archaic head
Kept singing after the body was torn away:
Body, old long companion, supporter—the mist

Of oranges, la-la-la, the smell of almonds,
The taste of olives, her woolen skirt. The great old
Poet said, What should we wear for the reading—necktie?

Or better no necktie, turtle-neck? The head
Afloat turns toward Apollo to sing and Apollo,
The cool-eyed rainbow lizard, plies the keys.

The Thicket

The winter they abandoned Long Point Village—
A dozen two-room houses of pine frames clad
With cedar faded to silver and, not much whiter
Or larger, the one-room church—they hauled it all
Down to the docks on sledges, and at high tide
Boats towed the houses as hulks across the harbor
To set them on the streets of Provincetown.
Today they're identified by blue tile plaques.
Forgotten the fruitless village, in broken wholes
Transported by a mad Yankee frugality
Sweating resolve that pickled the sea-black timbers.

The loathsome part of American Zen for me
Is in the Parable of the Raft: a traveler
Hacks it from driftwood tugged from the very current
That wedged it into the mud, and lashes it
With bitter roots he strips between his teeth.
And after the raft has carried him across
The torrent in his path, the teacher says,
The traveler doesn't lift the raft on his back
And lug it with him on his journey: oh no,
He leaves it there behind him, doesn't he?
There must be something spoiled in the translation—

Surely those old original warriors
And ruling-class officials and Shinto saints
Knew a forgetting heavier than that:

The timbers plunged in oblivion, hardened by salt;
Black, obdurate throne-shaped clump of ancient cane-spikes
At the raspberry thicket's heart; the immigrant
Vow not to carry humiliations of the old
Country to the new, but still infusing the segmented
Ingested berry encasing the seed, the scribble
Of red allegiances raked along your wrist;
Under it all, the dead thorns sharper than the green.

The Forgetting

The forgetting I notice most as I get older is really a form of memory:
The undergrowth of things unknown to you young, that I have forgotten.

Memory of so much crap, jumbled with so much that seems to matter.
Lieutenant Calley. Captain Easy. Mayling Soong. Sibby Sisti.

And all the forgettings that preceded my own: Baghdad, Egypt, Greece,
The Plains, centuries of lootings of antiquities. Obscure atrocities.

Imagine!—a big tent filled with mostly kids, yelling for poetry. In fact
It happened, I was there in New Jersey at the famous poetry show.

I used to wonder, what if the Baseball Hall of Fame overflowed
With too many thousands of greats all in time unremembered?

Hardly anybody can name all eight of their great-grandparents.
Can you? Will your children's grandchildren remember your name?

You'll see, you little young jerks: your favorite music and your political
Furors, too, will need to get sorted in dusty electronic corridors.

In 1972, Chou En-lai was asked the lasting effects of the French
Revolution: "Too soon to tell." Remember?—or was it Mao Tse-tung?

Poetry made of air strains to reach back to Begats and suspiring
Forward into air, grunting to beget the hungry or overfed Future.

Ezra Pound praises the Emperor who appointed a committee of scholars
To pick the best 450 Noh plays and destroy all the rest, the fascist.

The stand-up master Steven Wright says he thinks he suffers from
Both amnesia and déjà vu: "I feel like I have forgotten this before."

Who remembers the arguments when jurors gave Pound the only prize
For poetry awarded by the United States Government? Until then.

I was in the big tent when the guy read his poem about how the Jews
Were warned to get out of the Twin Towers before the planes hit.

The crowd was applauding and screaming, they were happy—it isn't
That they were anti-Semitic, or anything. They just weren't listening. Or

No, they were listening, but that certain way. In it comes, you hear it, and
That selfsame second you swallow it or expel it: an ecstasy of forgetting.

Louie Louie

I have heard of Black Irish but I never
Heard of White Catholic or White Jew.
I have heard of "Is Poetry Popular?" but I
Never heard of Lawrence Welk Drove
Sid Caesar Off Television.

I have heard of Kwanzaa but I have
Never heard of Bert Williams.
I have never heard of Will
Rogers or Roger Williams
Or Buck Rogers or Pearl Buck
Or Frank Buck or Frank
Merriwell At Yale.

I have heard of Yale but I never
Heard of George W. Bush.
I have heard of Harvard but I
Never heard of Numerus Clausus
Which sounds to me like
Some kind of Pig Latin.

I have heard of the Pig Boy.

I have never heard of the Beastie
Boys or the Scottsboro Boys but I
Have heard singing Boys, what
They were called I forget.

I have never heard America
Singing but I have heard of I
Hear America Singing, I think
It must have been a book
We had in school, I forget.

If the Dead Came Back

What if the dead came back not only
In the shape of your skull your mouth your hands
The voice inside your mouth the voice inside
Your skull the words in your ears the work in your hands,
What if they came back not only in surnames
Nicknames, names of dead settlement shtetl pueblo

Not only in cities fabled or condemned also countless dead
Peoples languages pantheons stupidities arts,
As we too in turn come back not only occulted
In legends like the conquerors' guilty whisperings about
Little People or Old Ones and not only in Indian angles
Of the cowboy's eyes and cheeks the Dakota molecules

Of his body and acquired antibodies, and in the lymphatic
Marshes where your little reed boat floats inches
Above the mud of oblivion O foundling in legends
The dead who know the future require a blood offering
Or your one hand accuses the other both lacking any
Sacrifice for the engendering appetites of the dead.

The Anniversary

We adore images, we like the spectacle
Of speed and size, the working of prodigious
Systems. So on television we watched

The terrible spectacle, repetitiously gazing
Until we were sick not only of the sight
Of our prodigious systems turned against us

But of the very systems of our watching.
The date became a word, an anniversary
We inscribed with meanings—who keep so few,

More likely to name an airport for an actor
Or athlete than "First of May" or "Fourth of July."
In the movies we dream up, our captured heroes

Tell the interrogator their commanding officer's name
Is Colonel Donald Duck—he writes it down, code
Of a lowbrow memory so assured it's nearly

Aristocratic. Some say the doomed firefighters
Before they hurried into the doomed towers wrote
Their Social Security numbers on their forearms.

We can imagine them kidding about it a little.
"No man is great if he thinks he is"—Will Rogers:
A kidder, a skeptic. A Cherokee, a survivor

Of expropriation. A roper, a card. Remembered
A while yet. He had turned sixteen the year
That Frederick Douglass died. Douglass was twelve

When Emily Dickinson was born. Is even Donald
Half-forgotten?—Who are the Americans, not
A people by blood or religion? As it turned out,

The donated blood not needed, except as meaning.
At a Sports Bar the night before, the guy
Who shaved off all his body hair and screamed

The name of God with his box cutter in his hand.
O Americans—as Marianne Moore would say,
Whence is our courage? Is what holds us together

A gluttonous dreamy thriving? Whence our being?
In the dark roots of our music, impudent and profound?
We inscribed God's name onto the dollar bill

In 1958, and who remembers why, among
Forgotten glyphs and meanings, the Deistic
Mystical and Masonic totems of the Founders:

The Eye afloat above the uncapped Pyramid,
Hexagram of Stars protecting the Eagle's head
From terror of pox, from plague and radiation.

The Western face of the pyramid is dark.
And if they blow up the Statue of Liberty—
Then the survivors might likely in grief, terror

And excess build a dozen more, or produce
A catchy song about it, its meaning as beyond
Meaning as those old symbols. The *wilds of thought*

Of Katharine Lee Bates: *Till selfish gain*
No longer stain the banner of the free. O
Beautiful for patriot dream that sees

Beyond the years, and Ray Charles singing it,
Alabaster cities, amber waves, purple majesties.
Thine every flaw. Thy liberty in law. O beautiful.

The Raelettes in sequins and high heels for a live
Performance—or in the studio to burn the record
In sneakers and headphones, engineers at soundboards,

Musicians, all concentrating, faces as grave with
What purpose as the harbor Statue herself, *O*
Beautiful for liberating strife: the broken

Shackles visible at her feet, her Elvis lips—
Liberty: not Abundance and not Beatitude—
Her enigmatic scowl, her spikey crown.

Newspaper

They make the paper with an invisible grain,
So you can tear straight down a vertical column.
But if you try to tear it crosswise, it rips
Out of control in jagged scallops and slashes.
Here amid columns is a man who handles
Search dogs. He says the dogs depend on rewards.
But not like the dogs I know, not dog treats: the Lab
Balancing one on his muzzle, trembling and gazing
Up at you till you say *"okay"* then he whips
The thing up into the air and snaps it and bolts it.
No, what the handler says is that his dogs
Are trained to find survivors—that's their reward,
Finding somebody alive is what they want.
And when they try and try and never get it,
They get depressed, he says: "These dogs are depressed."
Yes, what an animal thing depression is,
The craving for some redemption is like a thirst.
It's in us as we open the morning paper:
Fresh, fallible, plausible. It says the smoke
Is mostly not flesh or paper. First white, the drywall,
Then darker pulverized steel and granite and marble,
And then, long-smoldering toxic plastic and fiber.
How toxic, they don't know or it doesn't say.
In the old days, the printing plant and "the paper"
(Meaning the Globe or Herald or Journal or Times)
Were in one building, and the tremendous rolls
Of newsprint rumbled off the trucks each day.

When I was small one crushed a newsboy's legs.
There was a fund for him, I remember his picture
Accepting a powered wheelchair, in the paper—
Paper, the bread of Chronos, titanic Time
That eats its children: the one-way grain of downward
Irrevocable channels, the crosswise jumble,
Darkness innate in things. In the weather. In the boy
Who beams up at the camera or down at his stumps.
In the prisoner who speaks an unknown language
So that his captors guess and call him "the Chechen."
The errant, granular pulp. In some old stories,
The servant rises early and reads the paper,
Then gets the iron and presses it flat and smooth
To place by the master's breakfast—the skin of days.

Eurydice and Stalin

She crossed a bridge, and looking down she saw
The little Georgian boiling in a trench of blood.
He hailed her, and holding up his one good arm

He opened his palm to show her two pulpy seeds
Like droplets—one for each time she lost her life.
Then in a taunting voice he chanted some verses.

Poetry was popular in Hell, the shades
Recited lines they had memorized—forgetful
Even of who they were, but famished for life.

And who was she? The little scoundrel below her
Opened his palm again to show that the seeds
Had multiplied, with one for every month

He held her child hostage, or each false poem
He extorted from her. He smiled a curse and gestured
As though to offer her a quenching berry.

On certain pages of her printed books
She had glued new handwritten poems to cover
The ones she was ashamed of: now could he want

Credit as her patron, for those thickened pages?
He said she was the canary he had blinded
To make it sing. Her courage, so much birdseed.

Shame, endless revision, inexhaustible art:
The hunchback loves his hump. She crossed the bridge
And wandered across a field of steaming ashes.

Was it a government or an impassioned mob
That tore some poet to pieces? She struggled to recall
The name, and was it herself, a radiant O.

Akhmatova's "Summer Garden"

I want to return to that unique garden walled
By the most magnificent ironwork in the world

Where the statues remember me young and I remember
Them the year they were underwater

And in fragrant silence
Under a royal colonnade of lindens

I imagine the creaking of ships' masts and the swan
Floats across the centuries admiring its flawless twin.

Asleep there like the dead are hundreds of thousands
Of footfalls of friends and enemies, enemies and friends

The procession of those shades is endless
From the granite urn to the doorway of the palace

Where my white nights of those years whisper
About some love grand and mysterious

And everything glows like mother-of-pearl and jasper
Though the source of that light also is mysterious.

II

Thing

Thing, thyngan: *verb.*

From Old English *thyngian*, to parley, to assemble, to confer, to reach terms. To address, to give voice. Compare Old Norse *thyngan*: to hold a public meeting, and Old High German *dingôn*: to hold a court, to conduct a lawsuit, to negotiate a compromise or terms of peace.

Thing: *noun.*

Forms: **ðing, þinge, thyng, thinge, thynge.** [Old English *þing*; Old Frisian *thing, ting*]: assembly, council, lawsuit, matter. Old Saxon *thing*: an assembly, conference, transaction, matter, object.

Danish *ting*: a court of justice. Norwegian *ting*: a public assembly; also a creature, a being.

A spoken opinion; an idea; a thought.

A suit; a plaint; a decision; a discourse or a giving voice.

A convocation or parliament of voices.

The *thingstead* is the place of discussion or parley.

From an assembly or law court comes the sense of a matter at hand, an issue for debate. And from that sense comes eventually the nearly opposite sense of a concrete object, a physical or bodily thing.

First Things to Hand

1. First Things to Hand

In the skull kept on the desk.
In the spider-pod in the dust.

Or nowhere. In milkmaids, in loaves,
Or nowhere. And if Socrates leaves

His house in the morning,
When he returns in the evening

He will find Socrates waiting
On the doorstep. Buddha the stick

You use to clear the path,
And Buddha the dog-doo you flick

Away with it, nowhere or in each
Several thing you touch:

The dollar bill, the button
That works the television.

Even in the joke, the three
Words American men say

After making love. *Where's
The remote?* In the tears

In things, proximate, intimate.
In the wired stem with root

And leaf nowhere of this lamp:
Brass base, aura of illumination,

Enlightenment, shade of grief.
Odor of the lamp, brazen.

The mind waiting in the mind
As in the first thing to hand.

2. Book

Its leaves flutter, they thrive or wither, its outspread
Signatures like wings open to form the gutter.

The pages riffling brush my fingertips with their edges:
Whispering, erotic touch this hand knows from ages back.

What progress we have made, they are burning my books, not
Me, as once they would have done, said Freud in 1933.

A little later, the laugh was on him, on the Jews,
On his sisters. O people of the book, wanderers, *anderes*.

When we've wandered all our ways, said Ralegh, Time shuts up
The story of our days—Ralegh beheaded, his life like a book.

The sound *bk*: lips then palate, outward plosive to interior stop.
Bk, bch: the beech tree, pale wood incised with Germanic runes.

Enchanted wood. Glyphs and characters between boards.
The reader's dread of finishing a book, that loss of a world,

And also the reader's dread of beginning a book, becoming
Hostage to a new world, to some spirit or spirits unknown.

Look! What thy mind cannot contain you can commit
To these waste blanks. The jacket ripped, the spine cracked,

Still it arouses me, torn crippled god like Loki the schemer
As the book of Lancelot aroused Paolo and Francesca

Who cling together even in Hell, O passionate, so we read.
Love that turns or torments or comforts me, love of the need

Of love, need for need, columns of characters that sting
Sometimes deeper than any music or movie or picture,

Deeper sometimes even than one body touching another.
And the passion to make a book—passion of the writer

Smelling glue and ink, sensuous. The writer's dread of making
Another tombstone, my marker orderly in its place in the stacks.

Or to infiltrate and inhabit another soul, as a splinter of spirit
Pressed between pages like a wildflower, odorless, brittle.

3. Glass

Waterlike, with a little water
Still visible swirled in the bottom:

Earth changed by fire,
Shaped by breath or pressure.

Seemingly solid, a liquid
Sagging over centuries
As in the rippled panes
Of old buildings, Time's
Viscid pawprint.

Nearly invisible.
Tumbler. Distorting,
Breakable—the splinters
Can draw blood.

Craft of the glazier.
Ancestral totem substance:
My one grandfather
Washing store windows
With squeegee and bucket,
The other serving amber
Whiskey and clear gin over the counter,
His son my father
An optician, beveling lenses
On a stone wheel. The water

Dripping to cool the wheel
Fell milky in a pale
Sludge under the bench
Into a galvanized bucket
It was my job to empty by
Sloshing the ponderous
Blank mud into the toilet.

Obsidian, uncrystallized silicate.

Unstainable or stained.
Mirror glass, hour glass, dust:
Delicate, durable measure.

4. Jar of Pens

Sometimes the sight of them
Huddled in their cylindrical formation
Repels me: humble, erect,
Mute and expectant in their
Rinsed-out honey crock: my quiver
Of detached stingers. (Or, a bouquet
Of lies and intentions unspent.)

Pilots, drones, workers. The Queen is
Cross. Upright lodge
Of the toilworthy, gathered
At attention as though they believe
All the ink in the world could
Cover the first syllable
Of one heart's confusion.

This fat fountain pen wishes
In its elastic heart
That I were the farm boy
Whose illiterate father
Rescued it out of the privy
After it fell from the boy's pants:
The man digging in boots
By lanternlight, down in the pit.

Another pen strains to call back
The characters of the thousand

World languages dead since 1900,
Curlicues, fiddleheads, brushstroke
Splashes and arabesques:
Footprints of extinct species.

The father hosed down his boots
And leaving them in the barn
With his pants and shirt
Came into the kitchen,
Holding the little retrieved
Symbol of symbol-making.

O brood of line-scratchers, plastic
Scabbards of the soul, you have
Outlived the sword—talons and
Wingfeathers for the hand.

5. Photograph

Light-inscribed
Likeness

Vulnerable to light,
To the oils of the hand.

The paper sensitive
The dyes ephemeral

The very medium
A trace of absences.

Speed of the years
Speed of the shutter.

The child's father
Crouches level to her

With the camera and so
She crouches too.

Agile the dancer.
Little room

Of the camera, wide
Gaze of exposure—

Shiva the maker
Shiva the destroyer:

The flash of your hammer
Fashions the shelter.

6. Other Hand

The lesser twin,
The one whose accomplishments
And privileges are unshowy: getting to touch
The tattoo on my right shoulder.
Wearing the mitt.

I feel its familiar weight and textures
As the adroit one rests against it for a moment.
They twine fingers.

Lefty continues to experience considerable
Difficulty expressing himself clearly
And correctly in writing.

Comparison with his brother prevents him
From putting forth his best effort.

Yet this halt one too has felt a breast, thigh,
Clasped an ankle or most intimate
Of all, the fingers of a hand.

And possibly his trembling touch,
As less merely adept and confident,
Is subtly the more welcome of the two.

In the Elysian Fields, where every defect
Will be compensated and the last

Will be first, this one will lead skillfully
While the other will assist.

And as my shadow stalks that underworld
The right hand too will rejoice—released
From its long burden of expectation:
The yoke of dexterity finally laid to rest.

7. Door

The cat cries for me from the other side.
It is beyond her to work this device
That I open and cross and close
With such ease when I mean to work.

Its four panels form a cross—the rood,
Impaling gatepost of redemption.
The rod, a dividing pike or pale
Mounted and hinged to swing between

One way or place and another, meow.
Between the January vulva of birth
And the January of death's door
There are so many to negotiate,

Closed or flung open or ajar, valves
Of attention. O kitty, If the doors
Of perception were cleansed
All things would appear as they are,

Infinite. Come in, darling, drowse
Comfortably near my feet, I will click
The barrier closed again behind you, O
Sister will, fellow mortal, here we are.

Pliers

What is the origin of this despair I feel
When I feel
I've lost my grip, can't manage a thing?

Thing
That means a clutch of contending voices—
So my voice:

When my mongrel palate, tongue, teeth, breath
Breathe
Out the noise *thing* I become host and guest

Of ghosts:
Angles, Picts, Romans, Celts, Norsemen,
Normans,

Pincers of English the conquered embrace.
Embrace
Of the woman who strangled her sister one night,

All night
Moaning with the body held in her arms.
The arms

Of the pliers I squeeze hard squeeze its jaws
And my jaw
Clenches unwilled: brain helplessly implicated

In plaited
Filaments of muscle and nerve. In the enveloping
Grip of its evolution

Chambered in the skull, it cannot tell the tool
From the toiler
Primate who plies it. Purposeless despair

Spirits
The ape to its grapples, restless to devise.
In the vise-

Grip *Discontent*, the grasper's bent.

Banknote

Behind city walls, calm rituals of exile.
The Brazilian cleaner hums and sponges the table.
A civil quiet between us I will not break

By chanting my gratitude in broken Polish.
She has the courage to be my great-grandfather Ike.
Thanks to his passage a century ahead of hers

I get to sit at the table, I write the check.
To recite this to him through her would be foolish.
Her only language for now is Portuguese,

Though every week she knows more English words.
On the Brazilian equivalent of a dollar bill,
Not only a portrait of Drummond de Andrade

But an entire poem by him: nineteen lines.
It makes the dollar look—Philistine. The poem
Is about a poem he intends to write about

The single diamond made of all our lives.
From gluts, dearths. From markets, forced migrations.
Nossas vidas formam um só diamante.

Sicilian Archimedes could move this adamant
Prism that we form, if he could stand outside it.
Locked blind in the diamond, its billion cuts and facets,

Molecules in an obdurate equilibrium
Of pressures, we cannot see the shifting fire.
Words on the banknote; the banknote tints the words.

From Ruth the Moabite, her great-grandson David.
And from Ruth's sister Orpah, Goliath the gentile.
Signature graffiti sprayed on security shutters

In characters the corrugations disable:
In the unpeace, the breaking of the wards?
The pyramid eye envisions networks of cable,

Gulfs arched, wilderness paved. In the system
Of privilege and deprivation, the employed, the avid:
Fraught in the works, turning the gear of custom.

III

Rhyme

Air an instrument of the tongue,
The tongue an instrument
Of the body, the body
An instrument of spirit,
The spirit a being of the air.

A bird the medium of its song.
A song a world, a containment
Like a hotel room, ready
For us guests who inherit
Our compartment of time there.

In the Cornell box, among
Ephemera as its element,
The preserved bird—a study
In spontaneous elegy, the parrot
Art, mortal in its cornered sphere.

The room a stanza rung
In a laddered filament
Clambered by all the unsteady
Chambered voices that share it,
Each reciting *I too was here*—

In a room, a rhyme, a song.
In the box, in books: each element
An instrument, the body
Still straining to parrot
The spirit, a being of air.

In Defense of Allusion

The world is allusive. The mantis alludes to a twig
To deflect the starling, the starling is a little stare
Alluded to by Shakespeare: Jacques-Pierre,

His name alluding not to spears or beers
Or shaking, though the mantis does tremble a little,
Helpless refugee. Or I imagine she does,

Feeding that fantasy to my heart, an organ
Alluded to by the expression "courage"
Like "Shakespeare" from the French, M. Jack-Peter.

They say his father was a secret Catholic,
The sort of thing that could get a person killed.
Religion is nearly always a terrible thing

And even allusion sometimes is full of harm—
Though it means *play*—as when the President promised
To defeat terrorism with a great crusade.

His writers doubtless didn't mean to allude
To the Christians, including Richard *Coeur de Lion*
And several bishops, who made Jerusalem's gutters

Run bloody not as an image or figure of speech.
Lion-Heart nestled in some writer's imagination,
Atremble, romantic, disguised. In every thing

A ghostly gesture toward some other. In Yeats's
"The Stare's Nest by My Window" the Catholic soldier
Trundled in his blood, the nestlings fed on grubs,

The heart grown brutal from feeding on fantasies.
The Crusaders killed how many thousands of Jews
Among the thousands of Muslims. I used to know

A high school student who was brilliant at French.
The family she stayed with one summer were very kind
Though their allusions to dirty Jews or Arabs

Did bother her. What curdled her love for their language
Was how unconscious it was, like humming a tune:
"You couldn't wipe them out, they breed like rats."

All the starlings in America are descended
From ones imported because a certain man
Wanted a park with every bird mentioned by Shakespeare.

The birds are a pest, they drive out native species
In the world's rivalrous web of exterminations
And propagating shadows, the net of being.

Veni, Creator Spiritus

Blessed is He who came to Earth as a Bull
And ravished our virgin mother and ran with her
Astride his back across the plains and mountains
Of the whole world. And when He came to Ocean,
He swam across with our mother on his back.
And in His wake the peoples of the world
Sailed trafficking in salt, oil, slaves and opal.
Hallowed be His name, who blesses the nations:
From the Middle Kingdom, gunpowder and Confucius.
From Europe, Dante and the Middle Passage.
Shiva is His lieutenant, and by His commandment
Odysseus brought the palm tree to California,
Tea to the Britons, opium to the Cantonese.
Horses, tobacco, tomatoes and gonorrhea
Coursed by His will between Old Worlds and New.
In the Old Market where children once were sold,
Pirated music and movies in every tongue,
Defying borders as Algebra trans-migrated
From Babylon to Egypt. At His beck
Empire gathers, diffuses, and in time disperses
Into the smoky Romance of its name.
And after the great defeat in Sicily
When thousands of Athenians were butchered
Down in the terrible quarries, and many were bound
And branded on the face with a horse's head,
Meaning *this man is a slave*, a few were spared
Because they could recite new choruses

By the tragedian Euripides, whose works
And fame had reached to Sicily—as willed
By the Holy One who loves blood sacrifice
And burnt offerings, commerce and the Arts.

The Dig

Under the ruins, a steel
Mirror, intended to expose
The true faces of governors.

Beneath that rubble,
Inscriptions: annals of
Atrocities of the righteous.

Still deeper, the submerged
Foundation, dream-dark piers
Of speech, a chamber of clouds:

Atomized parables
Of descent, exhaled syllables
Of workers, victors, victims,

Dead languages alive,
Contagions of dust, mute
Parliament of each thing.

Inman Square Incantation

Forgive us, we don't exactly believe or disbelieve
What the President tells us regarding the great issues
Of peace, justice and war—skeptical, but distracted

By the swarm of things. The young Romanian poet in LA:
She said, "In Romania, bums are just bums, but here
In America the bum pushes a cart loaded with his *things*."

With a mean elfin look one of the homeless carters
In Alfred Vellucci Park sometimes begs using
A stuffed dog, bear or bunny as a prop: the paper cup

Panhandled toward us passing marks puppetwise—
Can you spare a little for Teddy? Or *The Doggie's hungry*—
Crooning maternal parody, a wheedling mock-innocence.

The noseringed leather kids who haunt the T station seem
The reverse—feigned menace. But one bashed some black girls
On the train, using the kind of metal rod called an "asp."

Some money to feed the bunny? His little poetry reading.
And the plush animal a street sign among signs, his ad
For something more personal and abounding than just need.

His smirk knows a thing sharper than pity to block my way by
The brazen ten-foot tenor saxophone that marks *Ryles*,
To *Top Cleaners*, the bank machine and *Patel Quick Food Mart*.

The dictionary says that a *thing* is first of all an assembly.
Forgive the word "bums." Forgive "homeless," our sheepish
Euphemism. "Derelict" is better for these forsaken.

Across the street from *Cerveija e Vinhos* and *Boston Improv*,
The Romanesque firehouse's arches frame bas-reliefs
Of horse-drawn ladder & hose. Amid these signs of civic

Rescue and cleansing, diversion and provender, let's
Remember, you rat-faced beggar: I dislike you. Forgive me.
And if as I pass again from where I've been I choose to take

A dead president from my breast pocket where I stowed the thing
To put it in your cup, it isn't Charity, but superstition—a provisional
Wishful conspiring with the artist in you, son of a bitch, bastard.

The Great Nauset Buddha

Plundered from Hangkow by some Cabot or Saltonstall,
The great image is preserved by the same soil that conceals it.
On his hike of the Outer Cape, Thoreau leaned on its brow.
He calls the smile "as replete and ruthless as the sea."

If a vandal paints across the Buddha's lip *Life Is a Beach*,
The defacement affirms the First Noble Truth:
Life suffers. The paint after a few seasons weathers
And blurs to illegible serenity. All things change:

Sacredness dwelling in the profane or nowhere,
Sacred clam shack, sacred drag show. Sacred stink
Of whales that in suicidal delusion beach themselves,
Packed close in the shallows to be massacred:

One Cape man made a fortune leaning from a dory
To carve his initials into their live backs and claim
His "blackfish." Illusion the fortune, illusion the knife.
Illusion that says *illusion*. The stench of looted bodies

Poisoned the air from First Encounter Beach to Truro—
Thoreau fleeing it was amazed at Wellfleet lobstermen
Calmly at work offshore, inured, as unbothered
By that decay as the Buddha himself, the blackened

Figure of Enlightenment like an inverted lighthouse
Beckoning and warning in the dark Void, the inward
Beacon buried by shipwreck in the shifting wall
Of a sandy hollow near the mouth of the Pamet River.

Stupid Meditation on Peace

"He does not come to coo."
—Gerard Manley Hopkins

Insomniac monkey-mind ponders the Dove,
Symbol not only of Peace but sexual
Love, the couple nestled and brooding.

After coupling, the human animal needs
The woman safe for nine months and more.
But the man after his turbulent minute or two

Is expendable. Usefully rash, reckless
For defense, in his void of redundancy
Willing to death and destruction.

Monkey-mind envies the male Dove
Who equally with the female secretes
Pigeon-milk for the young from his throat.

For peace, send all human males between
Fourteen and twenty-five to school
On the Moon, or better yet Mars.

But women too are capable of Unpeace,
Yes, and we older men too, venom-throats.
Here's a great comic who says on our journey

We choose one of two tributaries: the River
Of Peace, or the River of Productivity.
The current of Art he says runs not between

Banks with birdsong in the fragrant shadows—
No, an artist must follow the stinks and rapids
Of the branch that drives millstones and dynamos.

Is peace merely a vacuum, the negative
Of creation, or the absence of war?
The teaching says Peace is a positive energy:

Still something in me resists that sweet milk,
My mind resembles my restless, inferior cousin
Who fires his shit in handfuls from his cage.

El Burro Es un Animal

Kids in the Dumb Class weren't allowed to enroll for French
So instead we learned the difference between *ser* and *estar*.

A yellow-haired midget father in a white suit cursed me for being
In his family tent-yard, where I had wandered. He was my size.

All a misunderstanding, we weren't that stupid. I was earning
Free tickets to the circus for helping set up chairs in the bigtop.

¿Es larga, la historia? The language of Cervantes and Góngora was
Suitable for *nosotros*, being *bobos*. There are two kinds of *being*.

Fidel Castro was staying at the Theresa Hotel in Harlem.
He brought live chickens to eat, because they were safe.

What *are* these fucking motherfucking kids doing here, God
Damn it to the son of a bitch fucking cocksucking Hell?

Ya las gaviotas abren sus alas para volar, the young swallows or gulls
Are opening their wings to fly. We were stupid. He was small.

He was a scowling angel all dressed in white, wingless, his hair,
I suppose it was dyed, like yellow candy over his pink forehead.

Was and was. When Salvador Allende was elected President, what
Was the name of that honorable general killed by the CIA?

Be the fucking Hell out of here you little shit sons of bitches, Jesus Christ, before I put my foot up your goddamned fucking asses.

You are sick, the door is closed, María is tired, the apple is still green. The apple is green, Juan is intelligent, she is serious, the story is long.

Immature Song

I have heard that adolescence is a recent invention,
A by-product of progress, one of Capitalism's

Suspended transitions between one state and another,
Like refugee camps, internment camps, like the Fields

Of Concentration in a campus catalogue. Summer
Camps for teenagers. When I was quite young

My miscomprehension was that "Concentration Camp"
Meant where the scorned were admonished to concentrate,

Humiliated: forbidden to let the mind wander away.
"Concentration" seemed just the kind of punitive euphemism

The adult world used to coerce, like the word "Citizenship"
On the report cards, graded along with disciplines like History,

English, Mathematics. Citizenship was a field or
Discipline in which for certain years I was awarded every

Marking period a "D" meaning Poor. Possibly my first political
Emotion was wishing they would call it Conduct, or Deportment.

The indefinitely suspended transition of the refugee camps
Must be a poor kind of refuge—subjected to capricious

Kindnesses and requirements and brutality, the unchampioned
Refugees kept between childhood and adulthood, having neither.

In the Holy Land for example, or in Mother Africa.
At that same time of my life when I heard the abbreviation

"DP" for Displaced Person I somehow mixed it up with
"DTs" for Delirium Tremens, both a kind of stumbling called

By a childish nickname. And you my poem, you are like
An adolescent: confused, awkward, self-preoccupied, vaguely

Rebellious in a way that lacks practical focus, moving without
Discipline from thing to thing. Do you disrespect Authority merely

Because it speaks so badly, because it deploys the lethal bromides
With a clumsy conviction that offends your delicate senses?—but if

Called on to argue such matters as the refugees you mumble and
Stammer, poor citizen, you get sullen, you sigh and you look away.

On a Line of Hart Crane's

"And obscure as that heaven of the Jews . . ."

In the rabbi's parable a lame one climbs
Onto a blind one's shoulders and together
They pluck the fruit of the garden of the Lord.

O body the blind one, O soul the lame one.
Soul that is never purely the soul, thank God.
The body purely the body only in Death.

Barney Cohen, Puritan mullah in the sixth grade,
Scowled at me O Little Town when I sang
The carols, and Robert you won't go to Heaven.

O Barney, where did you get that idea?
When we were in our twenties I heard he died,
In a strange accident involving LSD.

Body that trembled on the shoulders of the soul,
How still we see thee lie. Above thy deep
And dreamless sleep the silent stars go by.

Or do I misremember, and was it Barney
Whose body was attracted by the carol?
Was mine the priggish soul that scolded him

Away from those *traif* hymns, thy dark streets shineth?
Purity of Sheohl, dappled impurity of life—
The ancient Jewish community included

Many who were not Jewish, the *ger toshav*.
In the pre-Christian Empire, Greek-speaking gentiles
Joined the synagogue body without conversion.

Is anyone ever entirely in the synagogue,
O Little Town? Or ever entirely outside it?
When the great Maimonides temporizes upon

The nature of the Jewish resurrection,
A whirring of subtle wings, a storied shadow.
And if we lack a heaven shall we construct one—

With banisters of pearl, six-pointed stars
And cartoon harps? Or Milton's eternal shampoo?
With nectar pure his oozy locks he laves.

A generation named their children Milton
And Sidney and Herbert: names of a past and a future:
An old world on the shoulders of the new,

A new world on the shoulders of the old.
The convert Hopkins thanks God for dappled things.
Barney, I wish I could take you onto my shoulders

Into the Vilna Shul on Adams Street
Where an immigrant master carver from Ukraine,
Sam Katz, who specialized in merry-go-rounds

Has made a Holy Ark adorned with lightbulbs
And shapes like manes and tails. How silently
The wondrous gifts are given, the freckled-forth

Obscure inventions. Blessed is the dotted
And spotted tabernacle. O lame and blind—
O mottled town, that harbors our hopes and fears.

Work Song

Fascination that dries the sap out of Yeats's veins
And rends spontaneous joy out of his heart—with *art*,
Art not "dolts" or "management of men" the difficulty

Craved and admired more than pleasure, more
Than accomplishment certainly more than Eden.
Heroic fascination of an overwhelming difficulty:

Joan of Arc tortured to death by clergymen
And failure incidental as for Jackie Robinson engaging
At one and the same time two worthy difficulties.

Other athletes succeed and get rich and in attained
Leisure even in Eden or Gomorrah they seek the green
Fields of the idiocy Golf because it is reliably difficult.

Old joke *It has to be hard to be good.* Manipulable
Light of the Xbox for all its eviscerations or hoops
Like chess a grid of exploits adequately difficult.

Music is difficult poetry is difficult Odysseus most
Interesting of the Greeks fails to get his companions home
But he does engage many an interesting difficulty.

Love also is difficult as in "Adam's Curse": at the end
Like the Odyssey's outset failure failure as it emerges
Like the hollow moon the couple is having Difficulties.

Even the infant sated by the breast turns eagerly
Irritable to its measureless impossible chore like Beowulf
Down to the darkness with his old comrade the monster.

The Material

The moon-stirred volume of ocean sighed
Coconut tanning-oil and frozen custard.

Birch lions and dragons rode the merry-go-round.

A splinter of the herringbone cedar boardwalk
Might be teased from your finger with a steel
Needle purged of germs by a match's flame.

When the sliver was out they held it
Up to your eyes, with bits of your flesh or blood
Stuck to it. Some doctors believe it helps
To see your tumor or gallbladder floating in a jar.

If Nana sewed a button on my shirt while I
Was wearing it, she made me chew a bit
Of the same cotton thread to keep the stitches
From piercing the precious tissues of my heart.

On the Day of Atonement she sat upstairs.

The shul was within the sound of the Atlantic.

Across the street, Our Lady Star of the Sea
With the rumored mutable crackers and wine
Swathed in its shadows. Froth of Communion dresses.

Three round medallions filled the rainbow arc
Of our shul's jewel-colored Palladian
Window three stories tall, with three images:

The eight-branched lamp; the double tablets of law;
The Star of David:—Study, Obedience and Pride?
Or blessedness at Home, in Heaven and the World?

Eight and Two and Six inscrutable
As the narcotic English translation my eye
Might swim to from the phonetic surf of Hebrew.

Meaning secreted itself in the urgent uncomprehended
Syllables the cantor sobbed,
In the eight miniature gilded minarets,
Terra-cotta pilasters and three high double doors—
In the velvet and silver fittings
Of the Torah you kissed only by kissing the fringe
Of your tallis, then reaching to press
That fringe to the cloaked scroll.

It flirted and hid itself in names, Sol Tepper,
Manny Horn, Isador Moss. Iossel, the ever-smiling "simple"
Concentration-camp survivor they treated like a child—
Grinning, but his dark round eyes like pictures
Of the starved, the mutilated, orphans deprived of touch.

The same men called to the bima to pray by secret
Desert-names: Reuven ben Nachman, Moshe ben Yakov,
Yisrael ben Avraham, in wingtip shoes and neckties.

And with Nana upstairs Sophie Gorcey, Molly Joffe,
Suzy Diamond looking down from the balcony.

Nylons, hat feathers, double-breasted suits.
Prescribed times to rise or sit or when those recently
Bereaved were supposed to leave the building
Or remain, or enter again through the three doors
Framed by four Ionic columns.

The church the synagogue the boardwalk all razed now,
Merry-go-round carted off: temporary as gestures,
Icons expendable, less enduring than names.

Made things like garments. Means. Conduits,
Like the dark vaulted cylindrical tunnel that led under
Ocean Avenue between the pool at Chelsea Baths
And the beach, where people descended from the bright
Stucco pavilions into the dark round mouth,
Then padded out onto the beach broiling in the sun:

Passageway of shadow from one blinding glare
Into a greater one, walkway invisible under the traffic,
Black damp burrow of the real, leading
From incomprehensible brightness to brightness.

XYZ

The cross the fork the zigzag—a few straight lines
For pain, quandary and evasion, the last of signs.

Poem with Lines in Any Order

Sonny said *Then he shouldn't have given Molly the two more babies.*

Dave's sister and her husband adopted the baby, and that was Babe.

You can't live in the past.

Sure he was a tough guy but he was no hero.

Sonny and Toots went to live for a while with the Braegers.

It was a time when it seemed like everybody had a nickname.

Nobody can live in the future.

When Rose died having Babe, Dave came after the doctor with a gun.

Toots said *What would you expect, he was a young man, there she was.*

Sonny still a kid himself when Dave moved out on Molly.

The family gave him Rose's cousin Molly as a wife, to raise the children.

There's no way to just live in the present.

In their eighties Toots and Sonny still arguing about their father.

Dave living above the bar with Della and half the family.

The Wave

(*Virgil,* Georgics *III:237–244*)

As when far off in the middle of the ocean
A breast-shaped curve of wave begins to whiten
And rise above the surface, then rolling on
Gathers and gathers until it reaches land
Huge as a mountain and crashes among the rocks
With a prodigious roar, and what was deep
Comes churning up from the bottom in mighty swirls
Of sunken sand and living things and water—

So in the springtime every race of people
And all the creatures on earth or in the water,
Wild animals and flocks and all the birds
In all their painted colors,
                              all rush to charge
Into the fire that burns them: love moves them all.

Antique

I drowned in the fire of having you, I burned
In the river of not having you, we lived
Together for hours in a house of a thousand rooms
And we were parted for a thousand years.
Ten minutes ago we raised our children who cover
The earth and have forgotten that we existed.
It was not maya, it was not a ladder to perfection,
It was this cold sunlight falling on this warm earth.

When I turned you went to Hell. When your ship
Fled the battle I followed you and lost the world
Without regret but with stormy recriminations.
Someday far down that corridor of horror the future
Someone who buys this picture of you for the frame
At a stall in a dwindled city will study your face
And decide to harbor it for a little while longer
From the waters of anonymity, the acids of breath.

From the Last Canto of Paradise

(Paradiso XXXIII:46–48, 52–66)

As I drew nearer to the end of all desire,
I brought my longing's ardor to a final height,
Just as I ought. My vision, becoming pure,

Entered more and more the beam of that high light
That shines on its own truth. From then, my seeing
Became too large for speech, which fails at a sight

Beyond all boundaries, at memory's undoing—
As when the dreamer sees and after the dream
The passion endures, imprinted on his being

Though he can't recall the rest. I am the same:
Inside my heart, although my vision is almost
Entirely faded, droplets of its sweetness come

The way the sun dissolves the snow's crust—
The way, in the wind that stirred the light leaves,
The oracle that the Sibyl wrote was lost.

Note

The references and proper names in these poems do not intend that a reader rush to Google or an encyclopedia. "Sibby Sisti" and "numerus clausus" have meanings, but such phrases appear also for their quality of forgotten-ness, a quality that lives in varying, unstable relation to meaning.

I tend to use the dictionary primarily for words whose meaning I know, absorbing the ones I don't know for their color and smell, gradually. Following this principle, I discovered the information on page 29: that the word "thing" first meant an assembly, then the issue discussed, and then from that relatively abstract meaning came the modern sense of a concrete object. The slangy-sounding expressions "to have a thing about" or "the thing is" hark back to that interesting history. Every artifact, every natural object, with its ghostly wrapping of associations and meanings, begotten and forgotten, is a gathering of minds or contending voices: every thing is an invisible assembly.

In a way, the power of such a history is that it is forgotten. The very word "thing" itself is an artifact, with a secret shroud or aura: the word—any word—is an assembly of countless voices that have uttered it or thought about it or forgotten it.

Forgetting is never perfect, just as recall is never total: the list or the person's name or the poem or the phone number may be recalled in every detail, but never with the exact feeling it had. And conversely the details may be obliterated, but a feeling lingers on.

That is why the trite notion that Americans lack memory or historical awareness is unsatisfying. *How* might we lack it, severally and collectively? One doesn't need to be a Freudian to understand that memory and forgetting are partial, willful and involuntary, helpless and desperate, in mysterious measures. Forgetting is not mere absence. The repressed does not simply return, it transforms and abrogates, rising and plunging like a dolphin, or Proteus.

In the haunted ruin of my consciousness, or of my country, one of the mad voices is the voice of journalism, swallowing and regurgitating as it speaks the jumble of what I have heard of or not. The muddle of what I have merely heard of, and no more. Where in the mess is a true reflection, a lasting truth? Sometimes from the babble a kind of clarity emerges, a genius: great comics of the early twentieth century say the greatest of them was Bert Williams. I have heard him, and he is an angel of comic song. He is partly forgotten—partly because he was a black man, and partly because he found he could do his best work only in blackface.

"Louie Louie," the poem that refers to Bert Williams, was in earlier drafts titled "Heard" and "Forgetting" and "I Never Heard Of." A friend was mystified by the poem: how I could claim I had never heard of George W. Bush. What could I answer? That I liked saying I had not heard of him? That there was a time not long ago when we had not heard of him—a failed oilman rich-boy son fronting for a baseball team? That someday someone, indeed many people, will not have heard of him? That the poem was meant to be in part an appealing babble? Or an irritable and irritating babble?

And how can the poem name so many things it hasn't heard of? Because it is acting dumb, I suppose, in a smart-ass way involving the contradiction of naming what one has never heard of—clearly the name must have been heard at least once by whoever says "I never heard of it."

The same friend, when he came to accept the poem (in a later draft), suggested naming it after the magnetic, full and empty song by Richard Berry, first recorded by the Kingsmen. The song is an amazing thing; we have heard it, and we have heard of it. FBI agents investigated it and hallucinated a subversive understanding of its hard-to-understand words.

"Numerus clausus" is the traditional term for a quota limiting the number of Jews admitted to universities: first at schools in Poland and Russia and then later—into the nineteen sixties—at "elite" American private universities. The story is told most recently in Jerome Karabel's 2005 book, *The Chosen: The Hidden History of Admission and Exclusion at Harvard, Yale, and Princeton*. Sibby Sisti played shortstop and second base for the Boston Braves in the early nineteen fifties.

R.P.